NEGRO LEAGUE BASEBALL

NEGRO LEAGUE BASEBALL

Photographs *by* ERNEST C. WITHERS

FOREWORD *by* WILLIE MAYS   ESSAY *by* DANIEL WOLFF

EDITED *by* ANTONY DECANEAS

HARRY N. ABRAMS INC., PUBLISHERS

All photographs are reproduced courtesy of
Panopticon Gallery of Waltham, Massachusetts.

The Publisher wishes to acknowledge Daniel
Wolff for his assistance in the final selection of
photographs, for his contribution to the captions,
and for his introductory essay.

Frontispiece: Joe Black and Roy Campanella meet the fans,
on the dugout steps of Martin's Stadium, Memphis, mid 1950s

EDITOR: Christopher Sweet
EDITORIAL ASSISTANT: Sigi Nacson
DESIGNER: Richard Baker
PRODUCTION MANAGER: Jane Searle

Library of Congress Cataloging-in-Publication Data
Withers, Ernest C., 1922–
Negro league baseball / photographs, Ernest C.
Withers ; essay by Daniel Wolff ; foreword by
Willie Mays ; introduction by Ernest C. Withers ;
edited by Antony Decaneas.
p. cm.
Includes bibliographical references and index.
ISBN 0-8109-5585-7 (hardcover)
1. Negro leagues—Tennessee—Memphis—
Pictorial works. 2. Negro leagues—Tennessee—
Memphis—History. 3. Baseball—Tennessee—
Memphis—History—20th century. 4. Withers,
Ernest C., 1922- I. Decaneas, Antony. II. Title.

GV863.T4M4629 2004
796.357'64'08996073076819—dc22

2004005390

Printed and bound in China

10 9 8 7 6 5 4 3 2 1

Harry N. Abrams, Inc.
100 Fifth Avenue
New York, N.Y. 10011
www.abramsbooks.com

Abrams is a subsidiary of

LA MARTINIÈRE
GROUPE

Acknowledgments

ERNEST WITHERS HAS BEEN A GIFT TO MY LIFE. No words can express how grateful I am to him for sharing with me his love of life, his love of family, his love for his fellow people, and his love for how photographs Tell the Story. Ernest and his wife, Dorothy, have welcomed me into their home on numerous occasions while working on projects such as this book. Their support and guidance brought the project to fruition. Thank you.

Others whose help, vision, and enthusiasm also contributed to the realization of the book include: Christopher Sweet, editor at Harry N. Abrams, as well as Sigi Nacson; Bill Chapman, an undying enthusiast for Ernest Withers as a person and as a photographer, as well as for all things baseball; Daniel Wolff, a great writer and a friend; SABR/Society for American Baseball Research, with special thanks to Dick Clark, Larry Lester, and Sammy Miller; Paul Sneyd, printer at Panopticon whose deft touch brought the photos to life; Micah Mayes, Boris Samarov, and Mark Sandrof at Panopticon Gallery for their help in organizing, scanning, and for their printing expertise; and David Brewer, Executive Director, Rickwood Field in Birmingham, Alabama. ~ *Tony Decaneas*

THANKS TO ERNEST AND DOROTHY WITHERS; Tony Decaneas and the people at Panopticon Gallery; Christopher Sweet and Sigi Nacson; Bill Chapman; Dave Dawson; John Haddock; Joe Scott; Govoner Vaugh; Penny Wolfe; and Rick Swig. As well as the standard baseball reference works, Peter Marshall Ostenby's 1989 thesis, *Other games, other glory : the Memphis Red Sox and the trauma of integration, 1948-1955*, provided valuable help. Even with these resources, there are gaps and inevitable errors in identification, and corrections are welcome for a later edition. Finally, thanks to that historical line of baseball insight that begins with Maurice Wolff, extends through Jesse D. Wolff, and continues with Nathaniel Whalen. ~ *Daniel Wolff*

Foreword

I REMEMBER THESE PICTURES: I was there. Other people make a big deal about the history and all, but I was there.

There's one here of me with the Chattanooga Choo-Choos. I was sixteen then—and bored. 'Cause it rained and rained all that season. They started me at shortstop, but I threw too hard so they switched me to center. I threw harder than when I went into the majors. And, boy, could I run! Wish I could run like that today. And the pitchers knew I could hit, 'cause they'd try and knock me down. That's all I had to do: throw, run, and hit. You do that, you can play anywhere.

I remember we got to Dayton, and it was still raining, and we weren't getting paid because we were playing on the pc (for a percentage of the gate), so I told the manager my dad wanted me home. And he believed me. So home I went!

Then, after that, I played with the Barons. There's a picture of that here, too. I see Artie Wilson—he's still around—and Piper Davis: he was our manager. Playing at home, in Birmingham, was fun. And easy: I just kept hitting the ball. Man, we went to all these places: Pittsburgh to play the Crawfords, Newark to play the Eagles, Cincinnati, Cleveland, Philadelphia. I came home, and my friends in high school were studying these places in class—I knew them from my job!

The highlight of my Negro League career was the Little World Series in Memphis. 1948. I hit a double, and then Jim Zapp hit a home run, and we won the game.

It came easy to me. The Negro League was a chance to make a little money doing something I was good at. That's what these pictures are all about.

~ *Willie Mays*

The 1948 Birmingham Black Barons after defeating the Memphis Red Sox, Negro American League Champions, beneath the Martin's Stadium grandstands. Willie Mays is in the upper left corner between two teammates.

Introduction

I HOPE THAT THE CURRENT GENERATION will enjoy these memories of baseball in the early days. With great appreciation to you, I present my photographs of the Negro American League baseball. The likenesses of the players, team owners, the friends and fans of the game, and the parks they played in give an insight into the culture of those segregated times. Before integration, African-Americans flocked in great numbers to the Negro League games, and I came and documented it with my camera.

My legacy as a photographer covers many facets of life in the South from Civil Rights and public events to entertainment in black nightclubs and on Beale Street. Chronicling the Emmett Till murder trial, I published a pamphlet of pictures that told the story. As a photojournalist I photographed the Little Rock Nine, Martin Luther King's activities, and countless other news stories. These have been collected in shows, previous books, and archives. Rising stars of the Memphis music scene, such as B. B. King and Elvis, who I pho-

Ernest Withers shown with Dorothy, his loving wife of sixty-two years.

tographed along with hundreds who appeared on tour here in Memphis, have also been published elsewhere. The present book shows the result of the time I spent professionally and pleasurably viewing some of the greatest ballplayers that ever played.

My focus was on the Memphis Red Sox and they are the strength of this collection. I sold the photos to local fans and they were also bought and used in the promotion of games by men like Matty Brescia and Sam Brown. There were great baseball men like Dr. W. S. Martin, Dr. B. B. Martin, and Dr. A. T. Martin. The great teams were the Chicago American Giants and the Birmingham Black Barons, whose owner, Tom Hayes of Memphis, was a tough man to work for, but my hat remains off to him.

I have memories of Pepper "Rocking Chair" Bassett whose mother, Lucy Bassett, came from Baton Rouge, Louisiana. He was one of the great characters of the game, a great catcher and great ballplayer. It was my good fortune to shoot the last picture of Josh Gibson in uniform in the 1946 East-West Game in Chicago. Gibson was a phenomenal player. I saw so many baseball greats: Alex Radcliffe and his brother "Double Duty," Little Willie Wells, Larry Brown, and Verdell Mathis. I was present for the rise of the Baseball Hall of Famer Willie Mays. Ernie Banks, Larry Doby, and Jackie Robinson all came through Martin's Stadium in Memphis on tour.

It's also remarkable to me that so many of the older ballplayers, like Chet Brew, tutored me in the manner of a big brother. Hundreds of names I remember with affection during that period of Negro Baseball. I am touched, too, with the memory of being able to capture players such as the legendary Satchel Paige surrounded by my family.

For the tremendous legacy of the work ethic that my father, Arthur Earl Withers, endowed me with, I give thanks. I credit my stepmother, Minnie Withers, with giving me the discipline of paying attention to visual detail. She, a seamstress, would give me fabric samples to take to the store, charging me with matching thread color to cloth. This sharpened and trained my eye for my future occupation.

To my beloved wife Dorothy: I am grateful for your support. In the early days, trying to make a financial success of our business, Dorothy helped me enormously, letting me use the bathtub for processing photos, and afterward, she would arrange and dry the prints on the oven racks in the kitchen. She gave birth to seven sons and a daughter: Ernest C. Jr., Perry O'Neal, Clarence Earl, Wendell Jacob, Dedrick (Teddy) James, Dyral Lewis, Andrew Jerome, and Rosalind Duvall.

All of their efforts shaped me to create the pictures that document the social life of the early days of Memphis. Negro League baseball games were one of the ramifications of life in the South before integration. It is my pleasure that those pictures carry forward today the information of yesteryear for the viewer.

∼ Ernest C. Withers

Diamonds Within Diamonds:
Ernest Withers and the
Negro Leagues

"**N**OBODY REALLY KNEW ABOUT US," IS the way Clinton "Casey" Jones put it. Casey Jones was the regular catcher for the Negro League's Memphis Red Sox from the mid- to the late 1940s. "Oh, the black people around the country and the South, they knew about us," Jones continued, "but nobody else."

On one level, these photographs by the legendary Ernest Withers simply address that neglect: they cast a light on what had been hidden. There's Casey Jones, now, grinning as he crosses home plate. And there he is in another Withers's shot: arm cocked, mask thrown down, posed like a warrior on the infield dirt. At the time, white newspapers didn't print such images. As Withers succinctly recalls, "White folks didn't want to read about no black folks." And Negro newspapers reported on the Negro Leagues, but not regularly. "They didn't get no Sunday-to-Sunday pictures of ball games," as Withers says, "... that wasn't part of their journalistic workings."

As a result, fans and historians have had to piece together what black baseball looked like. We have pictures of the greats: Leroy "Satchel" Paige and Josh Gibson and even the turn-of-the-century founder of the Negro Leagues, Andrew "Rube" Foster. But few

Clinton "Casey" Jones, Jr., Memphis Red Sox catcher 1940–1950, Martin's Stadium.

photographers have produced the depth and the range of black baseball images that Ernest Withers shows us here—from owners to fans, from the playing fields to the nightclubs, from the game's stars to its unknowns. As a body of work, these photographs not only provide basic information; they also offer a multifaceted view of the world in which black baseball was played.

Look, for example, at Withers's classic portrait of Memphis pitcher Verdell Mathis shaking hands with Joe Scott (*pages 88–89*). Both Red Sox are grinning broadly, a tired-out teammate slumped behind them in the dugout, another hurrying across the frame. According to Scott, this is at the end of a marathon game in which both the lefty ace, Mathis, and the New York Cuban, David "Impo" Barnhill, had thrown fourteen innings of shutout ball. Scott finally won the pitchers' duel with a home run, and Withers has framed the aftermath: a universal moment of exhausted exhilaration.

Or, find Mathis again, this time in the dugout of the 1948 All-Star game at Chicago's Comiskey Park. These annual All-Star games were the highlight of the Negro League season and regularly drew 40,000 to 50,000 fans. In Withers's portrait, three Birmingham Barons stand to Mathis's left: shortstop Artie Wilson, manager and second baseman Lorenzo "Piper" Davis, and pitcher William Powell (*pages 12–13*). Those names mean nothing to most baseball fans today. And if they do, it's probably because that year's Birmingham team included a seventeen-year-old rookie they all called Buck, who went on to greatness as the Say Hey Kid, Willie Mays. But the men in this photograph have their own fame. Wilson hit .402 in 1948; he's been called "The Last .400 Hitter." The Boston Red Sox thought so much of the hard-hitting Davis they offered him more money than the New York Giants eventually paid for Mays. Maybe these players weren't well-known beyond the edges of this photograph—beyond the silhouettes in the upper grandstands—but Withers brings them to us as stars.

In the dugout, from left to right: Verdell Mathis, Artie Wilson, Lorenzo "Piper" Davis, William Powell, Gentry "Jeep" Jessup (wearing sunglasses). In the stands, just above Mathis: Dr. W. S. Martin and, to his right, Jose Colas. 1948 East-West All-Star Game, Comiskey Park, Chicago.

Or, check out the ladies celebrating outside the Kansas City stadium *(page 14)*. One pours herself a beer; another pours her date one. "They were the working staff at Nudie Butt's Café," Withers recalls, "on Hernando off of Beale." Madam Nudie's was a favorite Memphis eating spot for visiting ball clubs, and Withers can remember just which ballplayer was courting which waitress. In this photograph, the women have taken a road trip to Missouri, and they're celebrating. From the elegant straps of their high heels to their carefully coiffed hair, they reflect a whole culture's joy and pride.

Finally, take a moment to look at Withers's picture of a bench-clearing brawl with the Indianapolis Clowns *(pages 16-17)*. The photographer has gotten close enough for us to see the players' disgust as they mill around, hands on hips. In the background, the umpire has kept his mask on: either making it clear there will be no more discussion, or just protecting himself. Uniformed security guards have been called out to restore the peace. It's the kind of scene that's familiar to ball fans, black and white. But black and white is what makes the difference here. The players are black, so is the ump, but the security guards are white men. The Memphis Red Sox hired them "for crowd supervision," Withers recalls. "Wasn't no lot of fights," he adds. There couldn't be: the white power structure in the city would have ended Negro baseball if there had been regular trouble. The sport these photographs reveal was played in a segregated stadium in a segregated part of town in a segregated city, state, and nation: diamonds within diamonds.

In 1946, as Ernest Withers first began taking pictures of Negro baseball, that carefully tensed structure was about to collapse. The Brooklyn Dodgers had just signed Jackie Robinson. Many suspected the game was about to change; few guessed how quickly or completely. While volumes have been written on how integration transformed the major leagues, here, at the very beginning of his career, Withers found himself in the unique position of documenting the institution Jackie Robinson left behind—and doing so from the inside. So, finally, what glitters through these photographs isn't simply who these players were—or even what segregated America looked like—but how and why that world was changing.

When Ernest Withers came back home from active duty in World War II, the twenty-four-year-old already had a family of two. (He and his wife, the former Dorothy Curry, would go on to raise seven boys and a girl.) The logical and safest choice for a Negro

Fans outside Martin's Stadium, opening day. "These are the girls from Nudie Butt's Café at the ballgame.

veteran in Memphis was to try to get a job working within the city's patronage system. "Employment was civil service," is how Withers puts it. "My daddy had already paid a lady [to line up] a civil service job." But Withers's skill as a photographer—an interest that had begun in high school—had only increased with army training, and he was determined to set up his own commercial studio. Soon, he was making photographs of black Memphis: weddings, funerals, and anything else that helped pay the rent, including baseball.

TO APPRECIATE THE COMBINATION OF WARMTH and objectivity in these images, it helps to know that Withers wasn't going out to ball games as a fan, or as a journalist, but as a freelance commercial photographer. "I associate myself with a love of a community team," Withers explains today, "but I wasn't no big worrier about any sport.... I went because it was a way to make money. I wasn't leaning on baseball," he emphasizes. "If there was a big church affair, I didn't go to no baseball game!" Withers saw himself as part of what he calls "a new course of photographers.... There was a need," he continues, "for my service by the Martins."

The Martins were four light-skinned brothers who had taken over ownership of the Memphis Red Sox back in the 1920s. Dr. W. S. Martin, the eldest, established himself at the city's Collins Chapel Hospital. Dr. J. B. Martin ran the South Memphis Drug Store. Dr. A. T. Martin had his own practice, and Dr. B. B. Martin was a local dentist. "They made their living as practitioners in medicine, dentistry, pharmacy," Withers observes, "and baseball was an extracurricular economic syndrome.... It was always a business with them." Withers's portrait of the four brothers (*page 18*), standing at the railroad station in their boaters and double-breasted suits, documents their status as members of that minority within a minority who were allowed to accumulate capital.

To understand the world these photographs depict, we have to go back to the prewar years of Withers's childhood. Black baseball—like any other Negro business in Memphis—

Left to right: Dr. B. B. Martin, dentist, Memphis Red Sox business manager; Dr. A. T. Martin, general practitioner, officer with Memphis Red Sox; Dr. J. B. Martin, pharmacist, Republican political leader, president Negro American League, owner Memphis Red Sox until l940, owner Chicago American Giants l940–49; Dr. W. S. Martin, superintendent Collins Chapel Connectional Hospital, owner Memphis Red Sox.

existed through the dispensation of one man: Edward "Boss" Crump. Withers first became aware of the city's political boss when the photographer-to-be was working for a dollar a day as a drugstore delivery boy. As Withers tells the story, one Easter Saturday night, the white owner shouted, "Come in here, boy! Come around here and take these flowers up in this hospital for Mr. Crump." The black schoolboy's first surprise was when he was allowed in the main entrance. "We could never go in the front door of the Baptist hospital," he recalls. "Never!" Then, walking behind, he watched as all the white folk greeted this Mr. Crump by name. When Withers got home that night, his father explained whose flowers he'd been carrying and how Memphis really worked.

Boss Crump ran the city like a plantation owner, but to the Negroes who fled share-cropping for Beale Street, there was a crucial difference: Memphis wasn't a plantation. Crump allowed black people to earn a living and to set up their own businesses, from broth-els to banks. Inevitably, his political machine would then demand payback, but within that system African Americans could find a job. And men like the Martin brothers were even allowed to prosper.

Withers makes clear that the most innocent of these photographs—pitcher Joe Black posing with two giggly little girls *(page 169)*, or infielder Larry Cunningham waiting for a ground ball *(page 103)*—occur within this context. "I was raised up a seat duster," Withers carefully explains. "You know, at Russwood Park." Russwood was the home of the city's whites-only, Southern League baseball team, the Memphis Chicks. "Every day, they would have a group of five or six or ten of us go around and dust them seats all over the park. And they had a little two- or three-man crew known as the birdboys. When the birds got in there and messed on the seats, we have a little knife and a little bowl and we'd scrape it. We were birdboys."

When the game started, the birdboys would be allowed to stay and watch. "And the white folks," Withers continues, "used to say, 'Hit it in the coal pile!' That's where all the 'nig-gers' were: the Negro section of the park, in right field, way out there. They would say, 'Hit it in the coal pile!'

"People don't understand," he goes on, "I mean, Negroes wasn't licking to be with white folks, and white folks wasn't licking to be with Negroes. It was just a separate society."

Withers pauses, then looking back some seventy years, repeats his words slowly and carefully: "It ... was ... *a ... separate... system.*"

Within that system, the Martin brothers and the Red Sox prospered. In 1938, the Martins bought out one of their competitors, the Cincinnati Tigers, thus forming the nucleus of a team that won that season's Negro American League pennant. One of Withers's earliest baseball photos captures the Red Sox power lineup: the hitters in carefully arranged profile, leaning on their bats at a certain angle, front feet neatly placed just outside the lip of the dugout. On the far left is Neil Robinson, who came over in the Cincinnati deal and hit 54 home runs the following season. Robinson would end up compiling a .303 lifetime average over eighteen years, most of them in Memphis. Next to him, left fielder Cowan "Bubba" Hyde was one of the fastest men in baseball. When he arrived from Cincinnati, his speed and quick bat made him an ideal leadoff man. The poker-faced William "Nat" Rogers— also out of Cincinnati—played right field and, between his line drive hitting and precision bunting, would win the batting title in 1939. Elsewhere, Withers shows us other former Tigers: Olan "Jelly" Taylor, the flashy first-baseman, and Ted Radcliffe, a .300 hitter nicknamed "Double Duty" because he could both pitch and catch. (Radcliffe ended up leaving Memphis in a salary dispute, calling owner W. S. Martin, "the cheapest son-of-a-bitch ever lived." Which may explain why the Red Sox had trouble holding on to talent—and usually finished in the low-middle of the standings.)

When Ernest Withers arrived on the scene, baseball was arguably the largest black owned and operated business in the country, bringing in over $2 million annually. The young photographer went to work furnishing Dr. B. B. Martin with publicity shots for barnstorming flyers, calendars, and the occasional feature in the Negro press. Soon, he was going to most games and had become, in his words, "familiar with Negro baseball and knew all the stars." His wife, Dorothy, recalls how they'd dry a batch of pictures in their oven at home, and then her young husband would take them to the stadium at Wellington and Iowa Avenues. Fans would recognize Withers and wave him over to buy a team shot for a dollar, or have him make a portrait of them in their Sunday best. Between that and the Martins paying six or seven dollars per exposure, he could take in thirty-five dollars a day— on good days, as much as one hundred fifty dollars. Compare that to the Red Sox players

Left to right: Neil Robinson, Cowan "Bubba" Hyde, William "Nat" Rogers, Fred McDaniels, and Wyman "Red" Longley, early 1940s.

getting around three hundred dollars a month, and Withers saw his baseball photographs making "a lot of money."

The year 1946 was a particularly good one for the Negro Leagues and for the Red Sox in particular. The Memphis club played its first exhibition game of the season to over 6,000 fans. The opening day doubleheader against the Indianapolis Clowns drew over 8,000. And the crowds stayed healthy right through the season, with 6,330 watching the final Red Sox game against the Birmingham Black Barons. In a season like this, Dr. W. S. Martin told *The Sporting News,* the brothers would make "twenty-five thousand a year, maybe thirty to forty thousand." No wonder Negro League owners believed the 1946 season marked the beginning of even greater prosperity.

IN FACT, IT WAS THE BEGINNING OF THE END. At that year's East-West game, Withers captured the power of what had been in his portrait of Josh Gibson. Some fifty Negro journalists were milling around Comiskey Park, hoping to get a shot of the great star, when Gibson motioned Withers over. "For some reason he just responded to me. I was the only photographer that he let take his picture." The result is believed to be the last photograph of the legendary slugger in uniform. Gibson's death the following January signaled the end of the era when the finest African-American ballplayers were known only within their own community.

After the official 1946 season, major-league ace Bob Feller helped organize a September barnstorming tour. "A way to make some money that we lost during World War II," Feller recalls. Over twenty-seven days, Feller's white All-Stars played thirty-five games against Satchel Paige's Negro All-Stars. "Everywhere we played," Verdell Mathis remembered, "standing-room-only crowds!" The All Stars earned top dollar, plus, in Feller's words, "The American public could see how well they [Negro players] could compete with the major leaguers." The American public up north, that is. Jim Crow laws prevented Feller's team from

Josh Gibson at the 1946 East-West Game, Comiskey Park, Chicago.
This is the last picture of Josh Gibson in uniform.

playing Paige's below the Mason-Dixon line. Search Withers's baseball images, and the only white major leaguer you'll find is in a business suit: Lou Chiozza, a former infielder who retired to Memphis.

In fact, you can argue that the sport these photographs document is *not* the American pastime. Oh, it was three strikes you're out and nine players to a team, but as Withers says, "In those days, it was biblical living to be separate." Since at least the Black Sox scandal of 1919, the major leagues had marketed their game as respectable, sober, and organized. They called their fall classic the World Series—never mind what happened in Birmingham, or Memphis, or Havana. Their league followed a schedule and kept statistics. Their players were "professionals." In a segregated country, Negroes might hit a ball and run the bases, but they weren't allowed to aspire to that level of respectability.

Historians relate how Negro baseball was faster, looser, more daring than what was played in the majors. We can only get glimpses of that in these photographs. But take a look at Withers's portrait of Richard King, aka King Tut. There the man stands in baggy uniform, oversized checkered shoes, a whistle around his neck, a maraca in one hand and a pretty woman in the other. "He wasn't no ballplayer," Withers says. "He was a clown. [And] crazy as a devil!" Apologists have tried to downplay this aspect of the Negro Leagues, arguing that black baseball was essentially an imitation of the majors: "shadow ball." But the photographs of Tut with an oversized first-baseman's glove, spitting water at his teammate, Reese "Goose" Tatum, or posing with the midget, Bebop, reveal one extreme of a game that had invented its own culture—and was unabashedly about entertainment. King Tut performed with the Indianapolis Clowns: a team that featured first-rate ballplayers from catcher Sam Hairston to a young outfielder named Henry Aaron. But the Clowns' co-owner, Abe Saperstein, had also helped organize basketball's Harlem Globetrotters, and the two teams did business in much the same way: clowning brought in people, and fine athletes held their interest. When Tut would slide into a base and pretend to be knocked out, or Pepper Bassett would catch an inning sitting in a rocking chair, the crowd roared its approval. The American pastime was one of the many institutions that black people couldn't enter. But they could excel at it and transform it—and poke fun at it.

King Tut and fan, Martin's Stadium, 1940s.

Like the majors, the Negro Leagues kept statistics, but nobody pretended they were absolutely accurate. How could they be when a club like the Memphis Red Sox regularly barnstormed more than they played official games? Saturday and Sunday might be taken up trying to beat the Chicago American Giants. But on Monday, the team would get in the bus and start a string of exhibitions that took them down through Arkansas and Mississippi into Louisiana and Texas, challenging the best of the semipro teams on one dusty small-town diamond after another. "We might sleep in a bed two nights a week," the Red Sox smooth-fielding Marlin Carter told an interviewer, "and the rest of the time we'd sleep, eat, and live in the bus." While so-called legitimate baseball kept track of every pitch, a typical Negro League statistic—say, Carter's .294 batting average in 1946—only included league games. In a sense, that's what he hit *after* work.

In many ways, the freewheeling sport that Withers documented anticipates the major leagues of a half century later. Players regularly switched teams for better salaries, and owners pursued any and all promotions. The Negro Leagues didn't pretend to be a sacred national institution; it was a business. And fans were realistic about running into their heroes at after-hours clubs with the city's prettiest women. Like the swing bands of the 40s, such as Lionel Hampton's and Count Basie's, Negro ball teams traveled the "chitlin' circuit," playing mostly to their own people and ringing brilliant variations on white America's standard themes.

In that sense, the Negro Leagues didn't challenge white authority. They couldn't. In Memphis, that reality had been brought home in a brutal fashion back in 1940. Dr. J. B. Martin, by then the president of the Negro American League, had staged an unauthorized political rally at which Crump was denounced as the "Hitler and Mussolini in Shelby County." Within days, the white papers were attacking Dr. Martin, and the Memphis police were subjecting customers at his drugstore to full-body searches. "For after all," Crump told the papers, "this is a white man's country." The doctor had no choice but to leave his home and business behind, moving to Chicago. As Withers puts it, emphasizing each word, "Mr. Crump was the power of Memphis. That's why he ran Dr. Martin out."

In the Booker T. Washington tradition, most Negro League owners figured out a way to work within that system. Their prosperity was offered as proof that they were "the real leaders of the race," and that Negro institutions, while separate, could be equal. From that

Lloyd "Pepper" Bassett (also known as "Rocking Chair") played with the Ethiopian and Cincinnati Clowns in the 1942–43 season and with the Birmingham Black Barons from 1944 to 1952.

perspective, every image Withers made of a Negro team in freshly pressed uniforms, every photograph of a contract signing in a well-appointed office, every picture of a shiny team bus proclaimed what one African-American leader in Memphis called the "militant philosophy of black pride." Assuming this system would continue unchanged, the Martins decided to expand their operation. During the winter of 1947, they hired a white publicist, Matty Brescia, and announced major renovations to their ballpark. According to the *Memphis World*, Martin's Stadium was "a constant source of pride to all of Memphis." It was also a constant source of profit. Unlike most Negro League owners, the Martins owned their stadium, which meant they didn't have to lease from a major-league club or limit their team's schedule. Now, the doctors invested an additional quartermillion dollars in a new roof, seating, concession booths, and, under the left-field stands, dormitory-style barracks for Red Sox players who couldn't find a place to live in crowded Memphis.

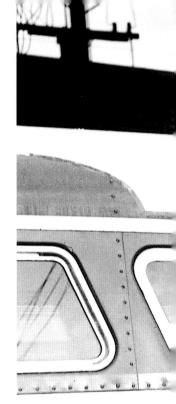

T HEN ON OPENING DAY 1947, JACKIE ROBINSON appeared in a Brooklyn Dodgers uniform. That June, Larry Doby became the first Negro to play in the white American League. The way the Martins and other Negro League owners read the news, integration was only going to improve business. For one thing, it would help publicize black baseball beyond its usual audience. And Negro fans would surely remain loyal. After all, that was part of the arrangement. As Dr. W. S. Martin wrote a fellow owner, "The people of Memphis have always been glad to help me in any enterprise I have been interested in." Withers's photographs reveal that, for a while anyway, the owners were right. He shows us the prosperous-looking Martins in the stands at the 1947 East-West game, along with their wives and successful friends. In another picture, we get to see Martin's Stadium with its new roof, its lights for night games, and the crowd so thick at an Easter Sunday doubleheader that it spreads right down the foul lines and out into left field.

"Baseball loomed higher when Jackie Robinson moved to the major leagues," as Withers

Unidentified player with the Memphis Red Sox team bus.

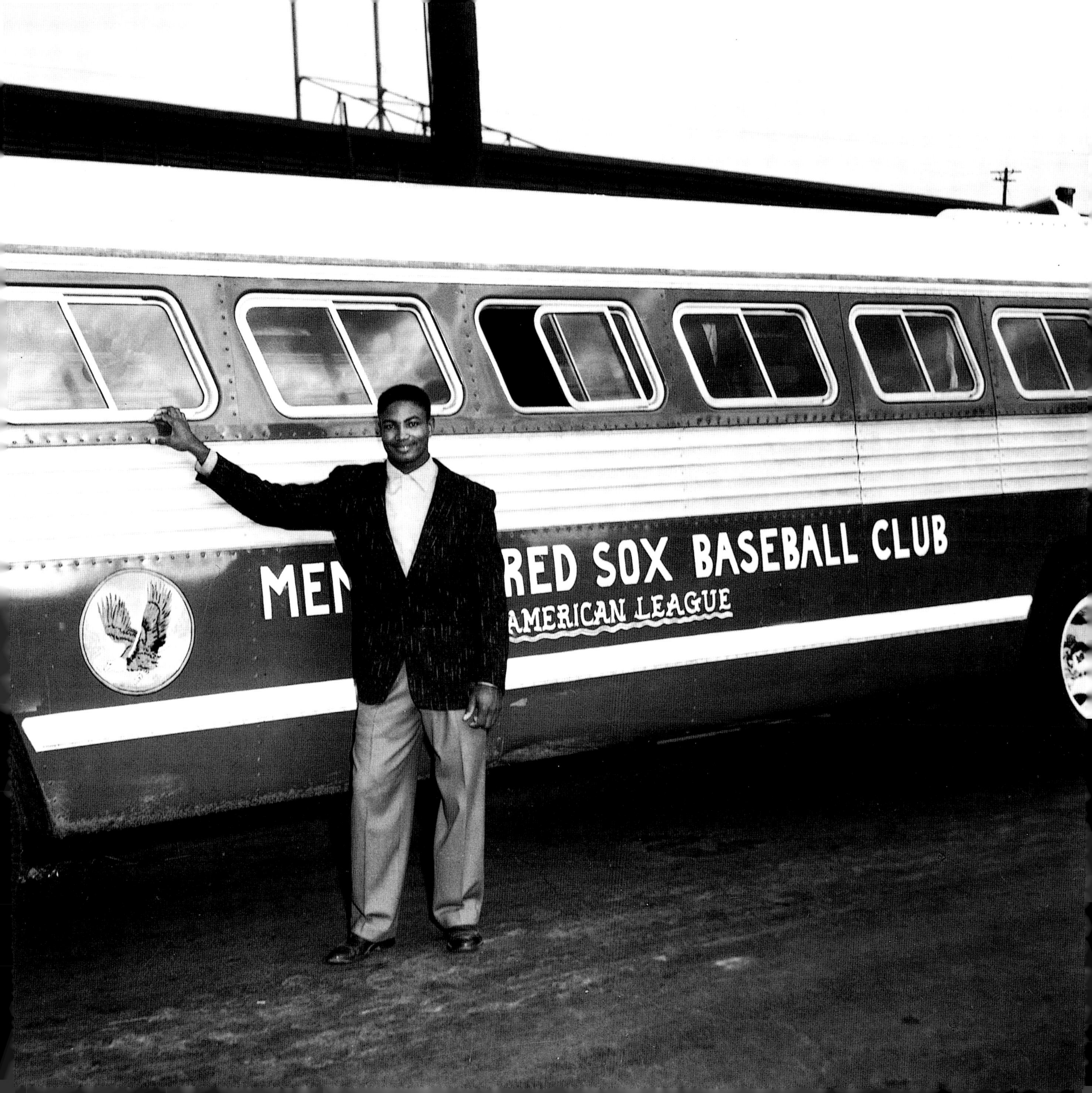

MEN
RED SOX BASEBALL CLUB
AMERICAN LEAGUE

says. "[It] got a cross-country, across-race elevation." Withers captured that change quite literally when he traveled to Sportsman's Park in St. Louis to see Robinson play. What appears to be an unremarkable image is taken from a perspective that, until then, had been unavailable to a Negro journalist: the press box in a major-league stadium. True, the day Withers strolled onto Ebbets Field in Brooklyn ("I went where events were going on, because I was an eventful photographer") the Dodgers's security guards, spotting a Negro amongst the other photographers, "lifted me off the field." But the change had begun. Between 1947 and 1953, six of the seven National League Rookies of the Year would be from the Negro Leagues, and, starting in 1949, nine of the eleven Most Valuable Players.

The other advantage that the Negro League owners saw in integration was an influx of new capital. Branch Rickey had managed to pick up Jackie Robinson without paying the Kansas City Monarchs. His explanation: "I have not a signed a player from what I regard as an organized league." But after that, Negro owners made sure all their players had legitimate contracts—the better to sell them off. Rickey had to pay the Baltimore Elite Giants for catcher Roy Campanella, the Newark Eagles for pitcher Don Newcombe, and, midway through the 1947 season, the Martins for their star pitcher, Dan Bankhead.

CONTRARY TO THE OWNERS' EXPECTATIONS, Negro fans across the country quickly began to switch their attention and allegiance to the majors. The Newark Eagles would report attendance of 120,000 in 1946, less than half that the next year, and only 35,000 by 1948. "Negro professional baseball is being killed," declared the Eagles' co-owner, Mrs. Effa Manley, and called on "newspaper fans, owners, and everyone interested in the welfare of our people [to] get together on a common basis." Tom Hayes, Jr., the Memphis undertaker who owned the Birmingham Black Barons, tried to rally support for "race conscious baseball." But even as they mouthed these words, the owners were busy auctioning off their best players to the highest white bidders. Why should fans be loyal to that?

Overflow seating at an Easter Sunday game, Martin's Stadium, late 1940.
Note white fans in lower left corner.

Elsewhere, Withers has documented the astonishing culture that African Americans managed to create within the white man's country: from the founding of the Church of God In Christ to the blues players on Beale Street. His extraordinary portraits of baseball fans underline the role that the Negro Leagues played in that culture. From the men in their wide-brimmed hats sitting in prime seats behind home plate—"Money-men" or "high-powered gamblers, card players," as Withers calls them—to the female "high steppers," Withers's pictures dissolve the simplistic, Saturday night/Sunday morning definition of black America. In the prime of the Negro Leagues, pool sharks sat side by side with saints of the church, brought together by the pleasure of watching one of the few public entertainments they were allowed: a good ball game.

But even as Withers reveals the rich complexity of segregated culture, he also shows how artificial and, ultimately, fragile it was. A generational, postwar change was at hand. In 1948, Boss Crump suffered his first electoral setback in over two decades: Crump's candidate for senator was defeated by a coalition of liberal white and Negro voters. Forced to make concessions, Crump hired the city's first African-American police officers. (Among them was Ernest Withers, supplementing his photographer's income to support a growing family.) *The Memphis World* reported that Beale Street was now openly discussing what had long been whispered: "The Negroes around here who are called leaders are hand-picked ... hand-picked by the white folk."

ITHERS'S EXPLANATION FOR THE sudden and successful integration of baseball is both matter-of-fact and mysterious: "Time migrated itself." Just as he sees separatism as the logical product of that particular era— "Baseball wasn't part of it; America and Memphis was!"—so he believes its rapid collapse was the inevitable outcome of changing times. Withers's night shot of Jackie Robinson on a barnstorming tour manages to capture the transition in both its glory and sadness.

From the press box in Sportsman's Park, St. Louis, 1947–48.

Left to right: Larry Brown, Mrs. Bob Boyd, Bob Boyd, Rufus Thomas, and Homer "Goose" Curry, Labelle's Café, Beale Street, Memphis, circa 1951.

By this time, Campanella, Newcombe, and Bankhead had gone to the Dodgers, Hank Thompson to the St. Louis Browns, and Monte Irvin to the New York Giants, among others. Withers finds Robinson sitting next to one of the players who didn't cross over: Larry Brown. "Historically strong with the Memphis Red Sox," as Withers puts it, Brown had joined the team in the 1920s and quickly become one of the game's finest defensive catchers. The story goes that he so impressed Ty Cobb, when they played together in the Cuban leagues, that the Georgia Peach had offered to pay Brown to learn Spanish. That way, the Negro could pass as Hispanic and join Cobb's Detroit Tigers. Instead, Brown played out his career in black baseball, including managing the Memphis team. Here, he crouches like the agile catcher he once was but in civvies, passed over. To Brown's right is "Luscious" Luke Easter in a Cleveland Indians uniform. Along with Satchel Paige, Easter represents one of the few older Negro stars who got a chance in the majors, hitting thirty-one homers in 1952 at the age of thirty-six. And there, on the left, is history's pivot man, Jackie Robinson, in a Dodgers uniform. He's staring at a clean white hardball as if it might hold the secrets to a shifting world.

"When Jackie Robinson went to the majors," Withers recalls, "the ballplayers began to recede out of Negro baseball. And the amateur leagues, they just could not beat the professional ballplayers. They just were not as talented...." Withers shows us those amateurs on the public diamonds in Memphis, but now these young players weren't dreaming of the Negro Leagues but of the majors. In 1950, the Martins sold their best hitter, Bob Boyd, for $15,000. From inside segregation, Withers gives us the before and after shots. There's Boyd as local hero: in a Red Sox uniform, at Martin's Stadium, shaking hands with disc jockey Dewey Phillips. When Withers finds him after he's been sold, he's in Labelle's Café on Beale Street, being welcomed back home by the Memphis music legend Rufus Thomas. Boyd is as popular as ever, except now he's working for the Chicago White Sox. And the profit taking has left the Martins without a competitive product.

Desperate, they began to recruit elsewhere. Many of the African Americans played winter ball in the Cuban and/or Mexican leagues. It was good money down there, but also, as "Double Duty" Radcliffe put it, "You'd be treated like a man." Now, the flow reversed. One of Withers's apparently routine portraits—seven smiling Red Sox lined up along a foul line

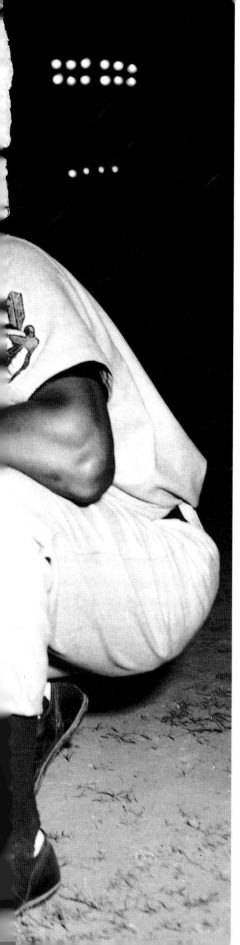

circa 1950 (*pages 38-39*)—actually offers a hidden message: Negro baseball had gone international. On the left is Panamanian-born Vibert Clarke, a fastballer who would eventually end up with the Washington Senators. Next to him is the charismatic Cuban slugger, Pedro Formental, who hit .347 with the Red Sox in 1949. The brothers Gilberto and Orlando Varona, infielders who learned the game in Havana, are followed by Cubans Jose Colas and Candido Mara. Finally, there's the Panamanian infielder, Edric "Leon" Kellman, who hit .329 for the Red Sox in 1950.

But this was, as Withers puts it, "in the latter part when baseball was fading out." By 1953, there were only four teams in the Negro American League. As the Dodgers' Roy Campanella was earning his second Most Valuable Player award and Junior Gilliam was winning Rookie of the Year, Withers's pictures of the Indianapolis Clowns start to include Toni Stone and Connie Morgan, women infielders hired to drum up business. Decent players, they were competing in a dying league. Kansas City Monarchs owner, Tom Baird, could urge Dr. W. S. Martin to "fire a pitcher or any player and hire a publicity man," but by now the owners couldn't afford regular salaries and were paying players with a (small) percentage of the (small) gate.

What did draw people to the parks were the All-Star exhibition matches scheduled at either end of the major-league season. Then, fans could see the men they'd been listening to on the radio. They knew Harry "Suitcase" Simpson from his time with the Philadelphia Stars, but now the power hitter played for the Cleveland Indians. The lean right-handed pitcher, Connie Johnson, had gone from the Kansas City Monarchs to the Chicago White Sox, and the six-foot-two-inch first baseman, George Crowe, now played for the Boston Braves, having broken in with the New York Black Yankees. Withers made a series of photographs of the All-Stars as they barnstormed from New Orleans to Chicago, playing local teams and celebrating the new day.

Left to right: Jackie Robinson, Larry Brown, and "Luscious" Luke Easter, Martin's Stadium, circa 1949.

WITH WHAT TALENT REMAINED, THE NEGRO
Leagues struggled on. In Withers's photographs, Frank "Groundhog" Thompson emerges
as a kind of emblem of this last, scrappy era. Josh Gibson had jokingly nominated
Groundhog to his "All Ugly Team." The tiny, five-foot-two-inch, one-hundred-thirty-five-
pound pitcher was walleyed and had what Withers calls "a flip lip." The crowd would laugh
when Groundhog first came out, but the lefty would soon silence them with his hard low
fastballs and good curve. In one of Withers's evocative portraits, shot below the Martin
Stadium grandstands, fans on both sides point toward the tiny pitcher, and Larry Brown
seems to be waving us closer with his rolled-up newspaper (*page 40*). Beside his wife in her
vibrant print dress, Groundhog stands as the calm, confident center of attention. The glory
days of the Negro Leagues may be over, he seems to say, but there's still some baseball
being played. (In the background, peeking out from behind the brim of Brown's hat, is a
right-handed pitcher who had a career before the leagues collapsed, then made it big as a
country-western singer: Charley Pride.)

The Memphis Red Sox lasted until 1960, when the team was sold and, as Withers
documents, Martin's Stadium was torn down. Though the photographer kept making baseball pictures till the end, his attention had shifted. Withers covered the Emmett Till trial in
1955, then the integration efforts in Little Rock and the emergence of Dr. Martin Luther
King, Jr., as a civil rights leader. In 1960, he photographed the Memphis sit-ins that were
finally forcing the city to integrate. "Separation," as Withers puts it, "was an arch enemy,"
and he acknowledges the contribution of Jackie Robinson and baseball in fighting it. At
the same time, Withers says, "I wasn't worried about no door openings." One of Withers's
last baseball pictures is the nearly iconic portrait of Jim "Mudcat" Grant, his confident grin
over the Indian caricature on his uniform (*page 183*). Grant is in the dugout at Russwood
Park where, long before, Withers had been a birdboy. On this Easter Sunday in 1960, as the

Left to right: Vibert Ernest Clarke, Pedro Formental, Gilberto Varona, Orlando Varona, Jose Colas, Candido Mara, Edric "Leon" Kellman, Martin's Stadium, circa 1948. As players left the Negro Leagues to enter the Major Leagues, Negro League teams sought new talent in Cuba and Panama.

photographer recalls it, "They wouldn't let me in the front. Because I was colored. Send me around to the colored gate." Laughing to himself—"It was the condition of *yesterday*; we didn't go home mad."—he nevertheless wished out loud that Russwood would just burn down. That night, the stadium caught fire and was reduced to ashes.

These PICTURES—MOST OF THEM NEVER BEFORE published—only add to the reputation of Ernest Withers as one of the premiere documentarians of the segregated South. Yet their lasting importance may lie in their unsentimental yet moving look at the closing down of that culture. There's the nineteen-year-old major league star-to-be, Elston Howard, the night he first put on a professional uniform. Beside him stands player/manager, John Jordan "Buck" O'Neil, who despite legendary skills never got a chance to star in integrated baseball. There's Willie Mays in the uniform of the amateur Chattanooga Choo Choos, the teenager poised and intent as if about to sprint for the Hall of Fame.

Finally, Withers finds the pioneers Jackie Robinson and Larry Doby standing together. Between them is the white publicity man, Matty Brescia, as if representing the business of baseball. Beyond, the fans sit waiting to witness history: most of them well-dressed African Americans but, off in the background, a section of whites, too. On the dugout steps, the kids beside Robinson know they're standing with a new American hero. But no one seems more intent than the young Kansas City Monarchs player sitting on the lip of the dugout just behind Doby. That's Ernie Banks before he made it to the Chicago Cubs and into baseball history. He looks out onto the field as if he can see the future coming. Thanks to Ernest Withers, so can we.

Frank "Groundhog" Thompson and his wife below the grandstands at Martin's Stadium, circa 1950.

Left to right: Ernie Banks (sitting), Larry Doby, Matty Brescia, Jackie Robinson, Martin's Stadium, 1953

The Claybrook Tigers. *Left to right, standing*: Leonard Henderson, Alfred Saylor, Dan Wilson, Bill "Wing" Ball (a one-armed player), Eggie Henley, Johnny Lyles; *middle row*: Theolic Smith, Walter Calhoun, Bill Tate, Jessie Askew; *front row*: Handful Davis, Bill Adams, Emmett Wilson. Circa 1935. *Ernest C. Withers Collection*. "**The high semi-pro league had that team, the Undertakers, that played against the Claybrook Tigers. John C. Claybrook owned the ballpark in Claybrook, Arkansas. He put a five-gallon can of whiskey on the first base line and a five gallon on the third base line. For the fans.... Mr. Fisher got down on his knees and said, "'Lord have mercy on this good corn whiskey!'"**

Previous page: The Memphis Red Sox.

Two photographs pinned to the wall at Ernest Withers's studio. The photograph above is thought to be the Undertakers team at Lewis Park, Memphis, early 1940s. *Ernest C. Withers Collection*.

Weaver brothers and fans behind home plate, Martin's Stadium, 1940s.

Joe Scott sliding into third, Martin's Stadium, 1948.

Martin's Stadium before the modernization, circa 1946.

Neil Robinson, Martin's Stadium, late 1940s. Center fielder Neil Robinson hit 54 home runs for the Memphis Red Sox in 1939, played in eight East-West games, and had a lifetime batting average of .303.

Umpires, East-West Game, Comiskey Park, 1946.

In the stands at the East-West Game, Comiskey Park, Chicago, 1946. *Left to right*, first row: unidentified woman, Dr. A. T. Martin, Dr. J. B. Martin, Mrs. Anderson Ross, Dr. Anderson Ross (future owner of the Birmingham Black Barons), Matty Brescia (p-r man), Dr. B. B. Martin; *second row*: Ernestine Martin (directly behind Dr. B.B. Martin) and Jose Colas (two seats to her right in white hat); *fifth row*: Robert Church, Jr., (in dark jacket and tie, on aisle, four rows up from A. P. and J. B. Martin). A bank president and member of the Memphis black upper class, he organized the first chapter of the N.A.A.C.P. in Memphis in 1917.

Pepper Sharpe, circa 1947. A right-handed pitcher, Sharpe went 8–3 for the Red Sox in 1947.

T. Brown, Martin's Stadium, circa 1946. "That's T. Brown. He was a great Red Sox ballplayer! In the early days. When I first started making pictures."

Memphis Red Sox, Martin's Stadium, circa 1946. *Left to right, standing*: Tut Lockman(?), Bonds(?), Jim Ford, unidentified, Fred Bankhead, Nat Rogers, Goose Curry, Larry Brown; *kneeling*: Ippy(?), unidentified, unidentified, Robert "Pepper" Sharpe. **"Jim Ford was a great ballplayer, mean as hell."** Ford reportedly attacked an umpire with a bat when playing with the Red Sox.

Unidentified, Martin's Stadium.

Unidentified, Martin's Stadium.

Mr. and Mrs. Charles Griffin, Martin's Stadium, mid-1940s. "**The Griffins were strong
fans. Their daughter married Al Jackson, Jr., drummer for Stax and Hi Records.**"

Larry Brown (far left) with fans, Martin's Stadium, mid 1940s. Brown was the star catcher for the Memphis Red Sox from 1938 to 1948 and became their manager.

Umpire Steve Boone, Martin's Stadium, mid-1940s. **"Steve Boone was a Beale Street pool player."**

Jimmy Newberry, 1940s. Newberry called his overhand curveball a "dipsy doodle."
In 1948, he went 14–5 with a 2.18 E.R.A. for the Birmingham Black Barons.

Left to right: Henry Merchant, unidentified, and Charlie Neal, Cincinnati Clowns, circa 1946.

Henry "Speed" Merchant, Martin's Stadium, circa 1946. Merchant was one of the fastest men in the Negro American League and in 1950, at age 32, he stole 45 bases in 80 games for the Indianapolis Clowns.

Fans in the stands at Martin's Stadium, late 1940s. "**That was just a Beale Street, Memphis roustabout.**"

Veteran Memphis Red Sox player Fields, visiting Martin's Stadium with his daughters. "**[Fields] was an early Red Sox, way before integration with baseball. He was in the old Memphis Red Sox.**"

Left to right: Perry Wilson, John "Buck" O'Neil, and Elston Howard, St. Louis, July 28, 1948. **"This was the first night that Elston Howard put on a major league baseball uniform."**

Richard "King Tut" King, Martin's Stadium, late 1940s. **"Tut and Goose Tatum were the early clowns and gave the advent to the Harlem Globetrotters."**

The Chattanooga Choo-Choos
at Martin's Stadium, circa
1946. Willie Mays, age 15, at
center, kneeling; John Britton
is standing, fourth from left.

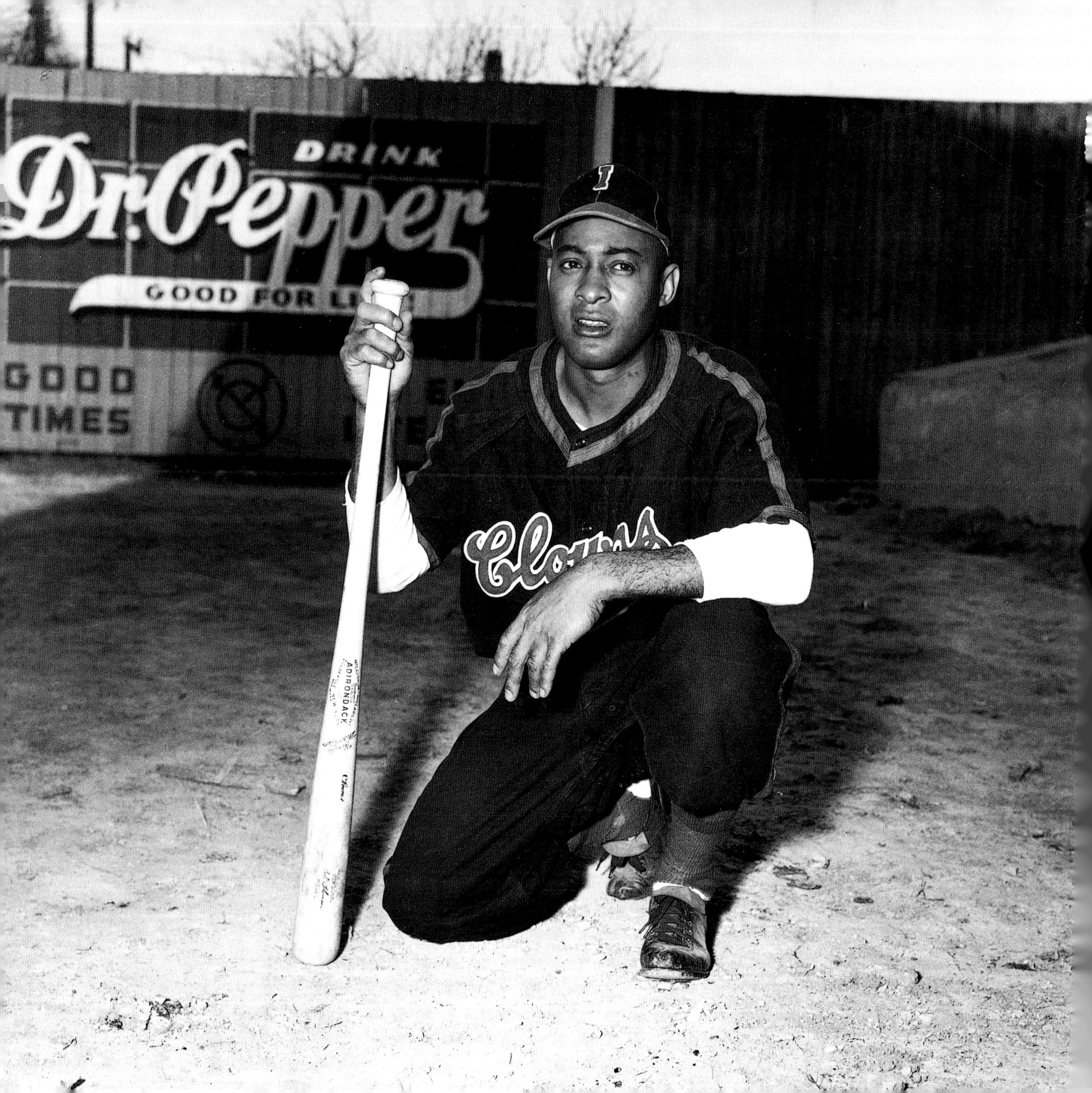
DRINK
Dr. Pepper
GOOD FOR
GOOD
TIMES
Clowns
ADIRONDACK

The Nudie Butts staff in the stands at Martin's Stadium, late 1940s.

John Britton, Martin's Stadium, circa 1950. Britton's act with the Clowns included shaving his head, wearing a wig, and then arguing with the umpire and throwing down both hat and wig. He was the first African American to play Japanese baseball.

GIs in the stands at Martin's Stadium, mid-1940s.

Piper Davis of the Birmingham Black Barons, circa 1948. As manager and second baseman with the Barons, Davis led the team to a league title and helped mentor their seventeen-year-old rookie, Willie Mays.

Dr. J. B. Martin and his wife at home.

Tom Hayes, owner of the Birmingham Black Barons, mid-1940s. The son of a successful mortuary owner in Memphis, Hayes bought the Barons in 1939 and sold them in 1950 after peddling Willie Mays to the New York Giants.

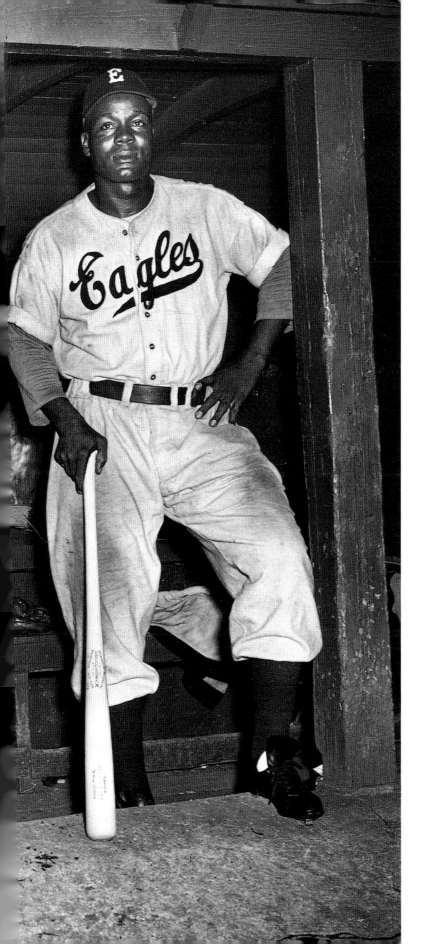

Left to right: Monte Irvin (shortstop), Len Hooker, Bob Harvey (outfield), and Len Pearson (first base) of the Newark Eagles, circa 1946.

Left to right: Sherwood Brewer, unidentified, John Britton, Sam Hairston, and Manuel Godinez of the Indianapolis Clowns, Martin's Stadium, circa 1947. **"They were top-notch ballplayers; there was no junk."**

The Memphis Red Sox with their team bus. *Left to right*: Sam Raif (driver), Larry Brown, Willie Wells, Sr., Joe Scott, Orlando Varona, Candido Mara, unidentified, Bubba Hyde, Willie Wells, Jr., Bob Boyd, Willie Hutchinson, unidentified, unidentified, Neil Robinson, Ernest "Spoon" Carter, unidentified, unidentified, Casey Jones, unidentified, and Leslie "Chin" Evans, circa 1948.

McKinley "Bunny" Downs in front with King Tut in back on the right. Indianapolis Clowns, Martin's Stadium, late 1940s.

Reese "Goose" Tatum on top (pumping) with King Tut on the bottom (spitting), Martin's Stadium, late 1940s. "When Tatum couldn't revive him, there's another picture where he stuck his foot in his face. When Tut smelled his stinky foot, he got up."

Behind home plate, Martin's Stadium, late 1940s. "**This [man] owned the Avalon poolroom....
These men were money men—high-powered gamblers, like. Cardplayers.**"

The Reverend Dwight "Gatemouth" Moore and his two sons,
Martin's Stadium, late 1940s. Gatemouth Moore, a blues
singer who returned to the church, was a regular disc jockey
and personality on the African American radio station, WDIA.

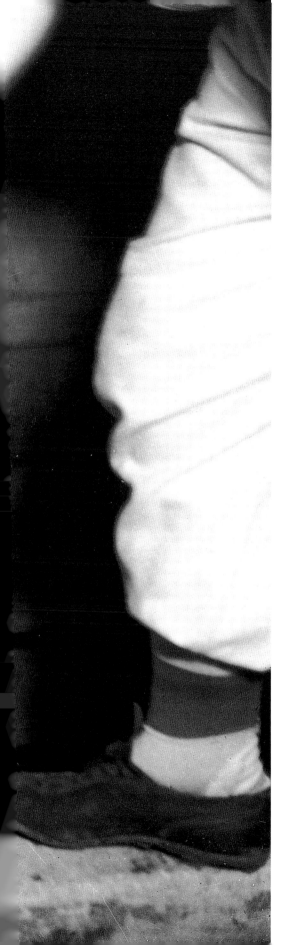

Verdell Mathis and Joe Scott, Martin's Stadium, late 1940s. Mathis, arguably the best left-handed pitcher in the postwar Negro Leagues, hurt his arm in 1947 and, despite treatment at Dr. W. S. Martin's Collins Chapel Hospital, never fully recovered.

Jackie Robinson and Bunny Downs under Martin's Stadium, circa 1948. "One of the reasons that we were hired as Negro police in Memphis is that Jackie Robinson made it to the major leagues. The white folk thought if a Negro could play baseball, he could also be a policeman."

Don Newcombe, Sportsman's Park, St. Louis, circa 1949. In 1949, Newcombe was Rookie of the Year for the Brooklyn Dodgers.

Roy Campanella, Memphis, late 1940s. Campanella was a star in the Negro Leagues—voted East-West MVP in 1941—and joined the Brooklyn Dodgers in 1948.

Left to right: Charles Tisdale, Monte Irvin, and Lou Chiozza, circa 1950. The outspoken Tisdale was a reporter for the *Chicago Defender* and became publisher of the *Jackson Advocate* (Miss.).

Monte Irvin, Sportsman's Park, St. Louis, circa 1950. In 1951, Irvin led the majors in RBIs.

Martin's Stadium after renovation, May 1954.
Ernest Withers's car is parked front and center.

Overflow crowd, Martin's Stadium, circa 1950.
"Oh, they had that crowd on Sunday!"

Bob Boyd shaking hands with Dewey Phillips, Casey Jones(?) catching,
Steve Boone umpiring, Martin's Stadium, late 1940s. Phillips was
the first disc jockey to play an Elvis Presley record, on WHBQ Memphis.

Casey Jones, Martin's Stadium, late 1940s.

Larry Cunningham, Martin's Stadium, circa 1950.

The Chicago American Giants, Martin's Stadium, 1949. *Standing*: Ted "Double-Duty" Radcliffe (second from left), John Miles (fifth from right), Art Pennington (third from right). *Kneeling*: Ducky Davenport (third from left), Theolic Smith (in the middle), Lonnie Summers (fourth from right), Gready McKinnis (third from right), Winfield Welch (far right).

Satchel Paige and the Withers boys, circa 1955.

Left to right: Perry Withers, Ernest Withers, Jr., Teddy Withers, Satchel Paige, Wendell Withers, and Clarence Earl Withers, Martin's Stadium, circa 1955. **"That's really in the bosom of greatness!"**

Fans at Martin's Stadium, late 1940s. The children in the second row
are Perry Withers, Clarence Earl Withers, and Ernest Withers, Jr.

Left to right: Goose Curry, Jesse "Hoss" Walker, Red Longley, Steve Boone, Martin's Stadium, circa 1950.

Sam Hairston, Martin's Stadium, late 1940s. Hairston
was the first African American to play with the
Chicago White Sox. His son, Jerry, and grandson,
Jerry, Jr., both played in the major leagues.

Ralph "Bebop" Bell and unidentified, Indianapolis Clowns, circa 1950.

Left to right: Ollie Brantley, pitcher; Isaiah Harris, pitcher; Joe Henry, pitcher; and Larry Cunningham, outfielder. Martin's Stadium, circa 1950.

"Rocking Chair" Bassett, Martin's Stadium, 1950s.

Willie Mays as a New York Giant.

Left to right: Hank Thompson, Harry "Suitcase" Simpson, Larry Doby, Roy Campanella, George Crowe, Monte Irvin, unidentified New York Cubans, Verdell Mathis (third from right). Martin's Stadium, 1952. "**They didn't have a bona fide umpire [at a barnstorming game], and I was asked to stand in. I called a strike on Monte Irvin. He turned around and said, 'You don't know nothing about baseball. You just here. Don't be calling no damn strike!' I couldn't put him out of the game.**"

CAMPANELLA
ALL STARS
1952

WITHERS
MEMPHIS

Roy Campanella and fans, Martin's Stadium, circa
1952. In 1951, Campanella hit .325 and was
the Most Valuable Player in the National League.

Ed Steele and Joe Black, Martin's Stadium, circa 1952. *In back, left to
right*: Charley Pride, Bill Little, unidentified, and Larry Brown.

Left to right: George Crowe, Joe Black, Hank Thompson, Sam Jethroe, Larry Doby, Roy Campanella, Monte Irvin, and Suitcase Simpson. Pelican's Stadium, New Orleans, circa 1952. **"I drove the bus with the major league All Stars leaving Birmingham once. The bus driver got tired and asked me could I drive. I drove from Birmingham to Greenwood, Miss. It would have been tragic if I'd had a wreck, but I was sane enough to just drive on the highway."**

Circa 1950.

Late 1940s.

1950s.

1950s.

The Memphis Red Sox. 1940s

Joe Black and Rufus Thomas, the Memphis disc jockey and record-
ing star, and his son, Marvel Thomas. Martin's Stadium, circa 1952.

Left to right: Milton Kelly (?),
unidentified fan, Marshall
Bridges, and unidentified.
Martin's Stadium, circa
1951. "**Harry Caray [the St.
Louis announcer]** used to
say when **Marshall Bridges**
went in hunting, and the
rabbits heard he was in the
woods, if he raised his gun,
they'd fall dead! They
knowed they were dead."

Orlando Varona and Gilberto Varona outside Martin's Stadium, circa 1950.

Left to right: Jose Colas, Olan "Jelly" Taylor, Pedro Formental, Martin's Stadium, circa 1950.

Orlando and Gilberto Varona with lady friends at The Flamingo Club, Memphis, circa 1950. **"This is —'s wife, and this is —'s wife. If the husbands had seen these pictures, they'd have killed them ballplayers."**

Candido Mara and Orlando Varona (sliding), Martin's Stadium, circa 1951.

Willie Mays, Lou Chiozza, and Hank Thomson at the Lorraine Motel, Memphis, circa 1953. Chiozza, a former major leaguer, ran a liquor store in Memphis.

Don Newcombe, Lou Chiozza, and Roy Campanella at the Lorraine Motel, Memphis, circa 1953. The Lorraine was one of the few motels for blacks in Memphis. After Dr. Martin Luther King, Jr., was killed there, it became the National Civil Rights Museum.

Leon Kellman, Martin's Stadium, circa 1952.

Vibert Clarke, Martin's Stadium, circa 1952.

Saturnino Orestes Armas Arrieta "Minnie"
Minoso with an unidentified fan, Martin's
Stadium, circa 1952. Born in Havana,
Cuba, Minoso led the American League in
stolen bases in 1951, 1952, and 1953.

Jehosie "Jay" Heard (pitcher), 1950s.

Tom Baird, owner of the Kansas City Monarchs, and Ted Raspberry, owner of the Detroit Stars, Memphis airport, mid-1950s. "**Goose Tatum told me [Raspberry] was 'loaded.' Said he was 'loaded.' He had breakfast in New York, lunch in Chicago, dinner in Memphis. I don't know what his occupation was. He might have been in the numbers business. Policy.**"

Overleaf: The Detroit Stars outside Martin's Stadium, circa 1953.

In Dr. J. B. Martin's office, mid 1950s. *Left to right, standing:*
unidentified, Lucky Sharp (a Memphis school principal), Sam Brown
(sportswriter), Tom Baird, unidentified, unidentified, Dr. B. B.
Martin, Shortman(?), Rud(?) (bus driver for the Birmingham Black
Barons), J. D. Williams (fan), Goose Curry, Sue Bridgefolk(?);
seated: Dr. Anderson Ross (owner, Birmingham Black Barons),
Dr. W. S. Martin, Dr. J. B. Martin, Ted Raspberry, and Russ Cowan
(reporter, *Chicago Defender*).

Marcia "Toni" Stone and an unidentified teammate, Martin's Stadium, circa 1954.

Left to right: Bunny Downs(manager, Indianapolis Clowns), Ray Neil(?),
Toni Stone, Buster Haywood at Martin's Stadium, circa 1953. "**Bunny
Downs, he was a smart guy. Bunny Downs was a businessman. If a
man went from city to city managing a ball club, you can't be taking no
dummy!... It was a money operation, Negro baseball.**"

Rube Williams coming home
with his Indianapolis Clowns
teammates greeting him and
King Tut kneeling behind the
plate. Martin's Stadium, circa
1953. Ray Neil is number 22.

Connie Morgan, Martin's Stadium, circa 1954. Morgan
replaced Toni Stone on the Indianapolis Clowns
when Stone signed with the Kansas City Monarchs.

Goose Curry, Miss Memphis Red Sox 1954, Lyman Bostock,
Sr., Martin's Stadium, 1954. Bostock's son, Lyman Bostock,
Jr., went on to play in the major leagues.

Left to right: Larry Brown serving Bob Boyd and his wife at Labelle's Café, early 1950s.

Dr. W. S. Martin, Goose Curry, and Bob Boyd in Dr. Martin's office, early 1950s.

Left to right, standing: Bill Bruton, Junior Gilliam, Roy Campanella, Dr. J. B. Martin, Suitcase Simpson, Jim Pendleton, George Crowe, Don Newcombe, Joe Black, Connie Johnson; *kneeling:* Larry Doby, Dave Hoskins, Bob Boyd, Othello Renfroe, unidentified, and unidentified. Martin's Stadium, circa 1954.

Ollie Brantley, who played for the Bisbee-
Douglas Copper Kings, and Ernie Banks,
Russwood Park, 1955. The Bisbee team
was part of the Arizona-Mexican League.

Ollie Brantley, Martin's Stadium, 1950s.

Lawrence Shaw, Martin's Stadium, 1950s. "Lawrence Shaw was semipro. I played high school football with him."

Connie Morgan, Ralph "Bebop" Bell, and Willie Gaines, Martin's Stadium, 1954.

Left to right: unidentified, Abe Saperstein, Goose Tatum, and unidentified, 1950s. Abe Superstein was the owner of the Halem Globetrotters and the Indianapolis Clowns.

Left to right: Harlem Globetrotters Walter Dukes, Ermer Robinson, and Goose Tatum with Paul Hardy (bus driver and former catcher) and Larry Brown, Memphis, mid-1950s.

Charley Pride, Martin's Stadium, circa 1953.
After an injury, Charley Pride switched from
baseball to singing country western and scored
his first of some thirty Top-Ten singles in 1966.

Satchel Paige, Mid-South Coliseum, Memphis, 1950s.

Casey Jones crossing home plate, greeted by Candido Mara, Jose Colas, and Orlando Varona at Martin's Stadium, mid-1950s.

Left to right: Dr. W. S. Martin, Dr. Anderson Ross, Dr. J. B. Martin, and Ted Raspberry, circa 1955. Raspberry bought the Kansas City Monarchs from Tom Baird in 1955.

Joe Black in a Cincinnati Reds uniform with a couple of young fans, Martin's Stadium, 1955–56.

Previous page: The Willie Mays-Don Newcombe barnstorming team. *Left to right, standing:* Dr. W. S. Martin, Dr. J. B. Martin, Don Newcombe, Joe Black, George Crowe, Hank Aaron, Brooks Lawrence, Charlie White (catcher with the minor league Rochester Red Wings), Connie Johnson, Larry Doby, Louis Loudon (with the minor league New York Cubans), Johnson(?); *kneeling:* James "Junior" Gilliam, Hank Thompson, Willie Mays, Sam "Sad Sam" Jones, Gene Baker, Ernie Banks, Monte Irvin. Martin's Stadium, 1955. According to the *Memphis World*, this barnstorming team played mostly to empty seats during its southern tour.

The Memphis Red Sox Calendar, 1956. By 1956, the Negro American League consisted of only four teams: the Kansas City Monarchs ("KCM"), the Detroit Stars ("Dt. S"), the Birmingham Black Barons ("BBB"), and the Memphis Red Sox ("MRS").

Rufus Ligon, road manager of the Memphis Red Sox at Martin's Stadium, 1950s. "**He was a good man. Not very communicable, but a good man.**"

The semipro Warriors at Bellview Park, Memphis, 1950s.
"Bellview Park in the separatist days, now Jesse Turner Park."

Left to right: semipros J. D. Williams, Ulysses Hunt (standing), unidentified (kneeling), the Queen of the Semipro League, Jose Alexander (standing, a high school principal), an unidentified player (kneeling), and Johnson Salisbury. Bellview Park, late 1950s.

"Big" Bill Williams, 1950s. "**Big Bill Williams
was in semipro. That was when the Kansas City
Monarchs were scouting him.** He was with the
Bartlett team in Bartlett, Tennessee. **He played a
stinch with the Monarchs. I went to his funeral.**"

Unidentified Louisville players, Martin's Stadium, 1950s.

Chin Davis and his mother, Memphis, late 1950s. "**Chin Davis, he was a local amateur ballplayer that flirted in and out of the Negro League but never went in.**"

Joe Henry, Martin's Stadium, circa 1958. Henry, who came up as a pitcher for the Memphis Red Sox, eventually became known as Clown Prince Joe Henry with the Detroit Stars.

Dr. W. S. Martin's funeral, Collins Chapel, 1958. Dr. Wilkins is speaking.

Dr. W. S. Martin's funeral, Collins Chapel of the CME Church, Washington and Orleans, Memphis, 1958. "That's going into the church. That's **Frank Scott** (front pallbearer), **Larry Brown** (pallbearer in white suit), **Dr. Wilkins** (pallbearer at rear, in bow tie), and members of the **Masonic lodge. And M**emphis police officer **Shug Jones in the background. He dead; all them dead.**"

Marvel Thomas and Joe Henry. Memphis, late 1950s.

Jim "Mudcat" Grant, Russwood Park, April 17, 1960. The night Russwood Park burned down.

Previous page: Martin's Stadium being torn down to make way for a Mack truck distribution center, 1961.

Semipro Opening Day, Memphis, May 5, 1963.

The semipro Warriors, Bellview Park, Memphis, 1960s(?).

Negro League Reunion, The Pink Palace, Memphis, 1990s; *left to right*: Frank Pearson, Dr. V. Lane Rawlings, Joe Scott, Marlin Carter (seated), Jack Carpenter, Verdell Mathis.

Goose Curry and his family posing in Ernest Withers's studio, Memphis, August 7, 1963.

Index

Pages in *italics* indicate illustrations.

In the dugout, Martin's Stadium, circa 1950. *Standing, left to right*: Larry Cunningham, Buster Haywood, possibly Sam Jethroe of the Boston Braves, Marshall Bridges (?), and unidentified; *kneeling*: unidentified. Sam Jethroe debuted in the Negro Leagues in 1950 at the age of 32 and was named Rookie of the Year.